How to Make Money on eBay: International Sales

Taking the Fear and Guesswork Out of Doing Business Internationally on eBay

By Jill b.

© Copyright 2014
All Rights Reserved

ISBN: 1537466933
ISBN-13: 978-1537466934

CONTENTS

1	About this Book	3
2	Introduction	Pg 4
3	Who I Am	Pg 5
4	Shipping Internationally	Pg 7
5	Why You Should Sell Internationally to Maximize Profits	Pg 9
6	Our Neighbor & Ally: Canada	Pg 19
7	"It's the Economy, Stupid" -- The UK	Pg 22
8	A Road Less Traveled: Australia	Pg 27
9	Affluent Non English-Speaking Europe	Pg 31
10	Going South: Brazil	Pg 33
11	Selling Elsewhere	Pg 36
12	A Japanese Middleman	Pg 37
13	The Language Barrier	Pg 38
14	Currency Risk	Pg 39
15	Fraud Risk	Pg 42
16	Shipping Logistics & Risk	Pg 43
17	Describing Your Item for an International Sale	Pg 47
18	Conclusion	Pg 51

1 About this Book

This book is a supplemental guide to my first book: How to Sell on eBay: Selling on eBay for Maximum Profits. Sources, Tips and Secrets from a 16-year Veteran Powerseller. In this book, I will discuss how you can maximize profits by taking it a step further - selling internationally. This book is written such that it can be read as a standalone book. Some ideas in this book will apply to any seller, regardless of where they are located. However, the details of this book is specific to the US-based seller.

2 INTRODUCTION

Unfortunately, many US-based sellers are afraid of selling abroad. If you want to expand and sell more, you will need to look to further horizons for more arbitrage opportunities. By shipping internationally you will open up and increase your customer base tremendously. Something that is common where you live might be rare, valuable or difficult to get in another country.

Take videogame or movie memorabilia for example. When a popular movie is put on store shelves or when a game with a cult following is released, manufacturers often release exclusive memorabilia with the movie or game. Memorabilia can range from figures to books to trading cards and everything in between.

Sometimes, these collectibles are country-exclusive. They become even more rare if they are retailer exclusive. If it is something cool in very limited supply with a big cult following, you might have an international or even a domestic market (if it is popular and rare) for your item.

In my first eBay book, I discussed that arbitrage, as defined on Wikipedia, is "the practice of taking advantage of a price difference between two or more markets: striking a combination of matching deals that capitalize upon the imbalance, the profit being the difference between the market prices." Simply put: **buy low, sell high**. When you sell internationally, **you can sell higher**.

3 Who I Am

In 1998, I was a foreign student at Cornell looking for ways to make some extra money. In my home country, Singapore, the economy was still reeling from the 1997 Asian Financial Crisis. The 1998 US economy however, was booming. Americans were flushed with cash and were ready to spend freely. I found eBay. By 1998, eBay had already grown considerably. There was a large ready market in the US looking to buy unusual items online.

After some research (by checking eBay's Completed Listings), I found a small niche market in magazines featuring Asian actresses. I capitalized on my situation and made a small, quick profit from that niche. From this niche, I discovered another growing and much bigger niche - Japanese Anime.

Japanese Anime was the hot, cool new thing in the US. Anime however, had already been present in Singapore for almost two decades. Stores were clearing Anime toys out. By leveraging international arbitrage, and with my mother's help, I was able to make enough money in two years to cover tuition and all other expenses of my final two years at Cornell.

In the middle of my eBay selling career, I traveled around the world and found many items to sell on eBay. These sales either partially or fully subsidized my trips. Here is why I am in a unique position to write this book and why you should not fear shipping internationally. Here is a sample of my international selling expertise -

Countries where I have traveled to and found items to sell: Singapore (my home country), US (my adopted country), Canada, The Czech Republic, Slovakia, Hungary, Japan, China, Thailand, The Netherlands, Germany, Hong Kong and the UK.

Places I have shipped eBay orders *from*: Singapore, Calgary (Canada), Bangkok (Thailand), New York, New Mexico, Colorado and California.

Additionally, I have shipped countless items to all 50 states, as well as to many countries in six continents including the main English *and* French-speaking countries, Italy, Germany, Brazil, Peru, Ecuador, Saudi Arabia, the UAE, Israel, South Africa, Malaysia, China, Thailand, Japan, Indonesia, Taiwan, Hungary, Austria, Russia, Turkey and all the Scandinavian countries just to name a few off the top of my head.

4 SHIPPING INTERNATIONALLY

Before you decide on what you are going to sell, you have to know your shipping logistics. The most cost effective way to ship internationally is via the USPS. Unfortunately, since 2013, international shipping rates have gone up tremendously. I strongly suggest that you do NOT offer free or flat-rate shipping charges to international destinations.

Miscalculating the shipping charges to an overseas destination can be a very costly mistake. The best way to insulate yourself from any potential errors in your shipping quotes is to weight your entire package (box and packing material included) and have eBay calculate the cost for you based on the package weight and current USPS charges.

I like to pad the shipping weight by a few ounces to help cover any additional costs. In addition to that, I also usually add a reasonable handling charge of $1-$3 without any complaints from buyers.

When you are shipping internationally, shaving off every additional ounce counts. Make sure you do not use cardboard boxes that are excessively thick as it adds additional weight to the package. In most cases, as long as the item is not too heavy, use the cardboard boxes with the same kind of thickness that Amazon uses to ship their packages with. Boxes like these are sturdy without being excessively thick and heavy.

Save money by trimming down the inner box flaps (the shorter flaps - do not trim the long outer flaps). By trimming all four inner flaps you can save an average of 1 to 3 oz total - more if your box is bigger. Be sure not to trim it too close to the flap fold or you will render the box useless. A rule of thumb will be to leave about 1" of inner flap for small boxes, leave about 3" for big boxes.

To reduce weight, use bubble wrap, air packs or clean, dry old balled up plastic bags. Try to avoid using balled up newspaper or other kinds of paper as paper tends to be heavier than the plastic or styrofoam. Tape your package securely. Do not simply tape the flaps together. Your shipment may be traveling halfway around the world. Tape *around* all 3 dimensions of the the box - across, lengthwise and widthwise.

Follow the Money

At the time of writing in 2014, the US economy is unfortunately still weak. According to a Bloomberg report, "E-commerce revenue in China, India and Latin America were estimated to exceed $185 billion in 2012, increasing at rates as fast as 44 percent a year, compared with 14 percent growth in the U.S."

It is little wonder that in 2013, eBay started pushing for international expansion in BRIC (Brazil, Russia, India, China). So, the money is no longer in the US. It is time to expand beyond American shores.

5 Why You Should Sell Internationally to Maximize Profits

While there are some risks associated with selling internationally, I believe that the rewards far outweigh the risks. By selling internationally, you can not only open yourself up to different selling niches and opportunities, you can charge more for your items. To start selling internationally on eBay, simply opt to ship internationally. You can check off the countries that you want to exclude from your shipping regions.

When you start shipping internationally, you will find that some of your buyers may not actually be foreign. According to the US State Department, there are 3-6 million Americans living abroad. Depending on what you are selling, you may encounter an American abroad at the other end of the transaction. This means that the international market opens you to selling even the most mundane items. What is mundane to you may not be so mundane to someone else overseas.

Here's an example of a mundane American item: chocolate chips. I know it is an ordinary grocery item in the US but it is not so easy to get a hold of in Singapore (where I am originally from). If you can find it in Singapore, it is very expensive. I remember having to ask my aunt living in Canada to bring a pack of chocolate chips back from Canada whenever she came to visit so that I could make some chocolate chip cookies.

Years later, remembering this problem, I decided to resell some of those Costco-sized bags of chocolate chips when Costco had a coupon out for them. Verdict: They did sell for double what I had paid. I do not remember which country I shipped it to, I think it was somewhere in South America. It took a while to sell but it did sell.

The funny thing is, that that chocolate chip listing led a Swiss buyer to contact me with a strange request: he wanted me to help him get a hold of Armenian-style pulled mozzarella cheese. Yes. Cheese. Not the dry shelf-stable cheese but the kind you need to keep refrigerated. It is an uncommon cheese but was available in Colorado so we agreed on a price. I filled his order and shipped it to Switzerland. I fulfilled two orders for him. Luckily, the refrigeration issued worked out for him because it was winter at that time.

If you are wondering if I specialize in food, my answer is "no". I did not try selling more food items because I do not want to keep a stock of perishable food items in at home for resale. Food is, however, a good potential product for the international market. Processed food makes a better sale item. Bear in mind that certain countries may impose restrictions on certain food and/or animal/plant products so before you jump in with both feet, make sure what you are exporting will not cause you problems.

I have gone on and on about shipping silly food items but what else do foreign buyers want? It really depends. Electronics are always in demand in many countries. However, when you start selling abroad, you will start noticing that there are different buying trends in different countries. The British, I noticed, may buy and collect the oddest things including airline barf bags (unused of course) and more usual items like video game memorabilia; the Australians like American pop culture memorabilia, the Japanese like retro Anime items (from the '80s and '90s), the French like almost anything to do with fashion and perfume, Brazilians buy video games and the Germans and Israelis will buy a mish-mash mix of items.

How Do I Figure Out What To Sell Internationally?

In my first book, I discussed the simplest way to figure out what sells and for what price: simply use eBay's "Completed Listings" search. How then do you figure out what sells in another country and for what price?

The answer is simple and the process is free. On http://ebay.com, simply type in your item search and click on the "Completed Listings" (not the "Sold Listings") option. That pulls up the sales history for that item. For example, the URL for the search "iPad" in the "Completed Listings" looks like this:
http://www.ebay.com/sch/i.html?_from=R40&_sacat=0&_nkw=ipad&LH_Complete=1&rt=nc

Now, if I want to see what the demand and price for the iPad in the UK is, I change the "ebay.com" part to "ebay.co.uk" like this:
http://www.ebay.co.uk/sch/i.html?_from=R40&_sacat=0&_nkw=ipad&LH_Complete=1&rt=nc
that pulls up sales history of "iPad" available to the UK market.

Similarly, to check the sales history of "iPad" in Canada and Australia, I will change the URL respectively to:
http://www.ebay.ca/sch/i.html?_from=R40&_sacat=0&_nkw=ipad&LH_Complete=1&rt=nc
and
http://www.ebay.com.au/sch/i.html?_from=R40&_sacat=0&_nkw=ipad&LH_Complete=1&rt=nc

These are the biggest main English sites to consider. However, there are other non-English eBay sites like eBay Germany (http://ebay.de) that you might want to consider selling on. Except for the potential language differences, the search process is the same.

Being Aware of Compatibility Issues

Before you continue, you need to know that not everything that is made of the US market will work overseas. If you want to internationally, make sure that the items you sell will work overseas. Of course, a plush toy will function the same way no matter where it is. However, many other things are made to fit that region.

Electronic items, cell phones, video games, dvds and blu-rays are some examples that may not work overseas. Plugs and voltages are different in different countries; video games, dvds and blu-rays are often regionally coded and can only played in the region it was purchased in. You can refer to Wikipedia's reference list of electricity mains at http://bit.ly/1Ih6G8v.

Additionally, some countries may not allow certain items such as live plants or plant clippings, seeds, or certain food items to enter the country.

Since I do not always know what will work, I clearly state in my auctions that even though I will ship items internationally, the foreign buyer has the responsibility of checking to make sure the US item they are purchasing from me will work in their country. I bear no responsibility for incompatibility issues.

Opening Up Additional Arbitrage/ Niche Opportunities

In some cases, selling internationally can open up a niche for you that otherwise would not exist. In my first book, I discussed how you could leverage on arbitrage opportunities by selling local or regional items. The example I used was Ikea - the trendy Swedish mega-furniture store. People love Ikea's designs. Unfortunately for its fans, Ikea sells its furniture exclusively and rarely do they offer their items for sale online.

In the US, Ikea is located only in certain cities. People who live too far away from an Ikea would be willing to pay more to have someone purchase the item(s) for them and ship it to them. I had a repeat customer in another state that did just that - she would give me her Ikea shopping list and we would work out a small markup for my time and effort to get the items she wanted to her.

If you were to ship internationally, you could open up similar arbitrage opportunities that would not be available if you only shipped domestically. My short-lived Chumby (http://chumby.com) niche is a prime example of this. Chumby resembles a small clock radio with a digital touchscreen and WiFi connection. In addition to being a digital clock, I believe it could stream music and display digital photos. Wired Magazine named it one of the top gadgets in 2008.

To be honest, I am not sure what the device's full capabilities were. It did not matter. All that matters was that my buyers knew what it was and wanted it. So when Chumby was made available to be US public in early 2008, I was able to sell it to a ready foreign market. A LOT of it. I bought it at retail price and sold it for profit on the international market. I never had one US customer for my Chumbys. It would not have made sense for someone in the US to buy it from me, since they could easily buy it at the lower retail price directly from Chumby.

My arbitrage opportunity faded when Chumby itself started shipping overseas. It ceased operation in 2012 but may be revived by another company. Regardless, I was able to make quick, decent profits for a short while simply because I was willing to ship aboard.

My anecdote is US-based. However, the ideas can be applied to anyone living anywhere. Do you live in Japan and have easy access to beautifully crafted Japanese ceramics? Maybe (as a fictitious example,) there is a market for the new a green-tea flavored Cola only available in Japan? That might be a niche market for you. Maybe you live in the UK and can find a niche like selling canned mushy peas and Marmite to expatriate Brits living abroad. The possibilities are endless and, like my real-life chocolate chip example, can be unbelievably mundane in nature when you start expanding your selling horizons overseas.

Less Competition

Many US sellers will not ship internationally. That means, there is a much smaller supply of goods flowing into the overseas market. Let me use a simple, fictitious example.

Let's say that Apple has introduced the coolest new gadget - the iCool. The iCool has been released in the US and was a sold out item. Prices for the iCool on eBay are almost double the retail price. You, my savvy eBay reseller, has managed to get a hold of one of these iCools.

Can you make a profit selling it on eBay now? Sure, but what do you need to do if you want to make a bigger profit? If you also knew that the iCool will not be released internationally for another 6 months. Guess what? There is also a rabid Apple following in the UK.

These British consumers want to get their hands on the iCool before everyone else in the UK. A place that they will turn to is....eBay. You need to be at the forefront of such opportunities by selling to *them*. Since most US sellers will not ship overseas, you will be on the beneficial end of the short supply and high demand of British buyers. That means you can charge *more* than the other sellers. Sometimes MUCH more.

Higher Cost of Living in Other Countries

Many of your international eBay buyers will live in countries with a much higher cost of living than in the US. While Americans are used to big box stores full of cheap merchandise, many European, Australian, Asian and even Canadian buyers are using to paying higher prices for goods.

A fine personal example is when my mother comes to visit me from Singapore and marvels at how cheap just about everything is - from property to groceries to all the items I purchase for resale.

What does that mean for you as a US-based eBay seller? This means that not only would your foreign buyer, in general, be used to paying more than his average American counterpart, he/she will probably expect, and be willing to pay for that item that he/she is not able to get in his/her country. It means that you can charge your foreign buyer *more*.

Taking Advantage of the Weakened US Dollar

According to ForecastChart.com, over the last 10 years, the US Dollar has had a median decline of 12% against other currencies. In countries of specific interest, during that same period, the US Dollar declined by 24% against the Australian Dollar, it declined by 17% against the Canadian Dollar and by 9% against the Euro.

More information can be found at http://bit.ly/1obpOsD. The weakened US Dollar means that your foreign buyer is now spending less of their currency to buy your item.

You can take advantage of currency arbitrage no matter where you are. If you are based in the US, you can arbitrage by selling to countries which have stronger economies or currencies including the UK (British Pound Sterling), most of Europe (Euros), Canada and Australia (the Canadian and Australian Dollars are almost on par with the US$ but their cost of living tends to be higher).

Of course, you can ship to other countries as well. However, I've found that these are the main regions in the world that a big majority of my international customers have come from, probably because of the common language.

Let me turn my fictitious iCool example into a real world one to show how you can take advantage of currency differences to make money. Here's a real world example - the iPad Air which retails in the US at US$499. This product retails in the UK for £399 and is sold out in the UK. At the current exchange rate, £1 = US$1.63, the UK retail price is approximately US$652.

So, if you bought this iPad Air in the US for the full retail price of US$499 and sold it to someone in the UK for the UK retail price of £399 (US$652), your profit would be US$153 (to make it simpler to understand, I will not factor in taxes, ebay, paypal and shipping costs). If the iPad is in great demand in the UK, you might even be able to sell it at over the UK retail price and increase your profit.

With increased reward comes an additional element of risk. If you list your items in British Pound Sterling to maximize your sales potential in the UK market, there is a chance that your profit margin can diminish if the British Pound drops or plunges in value against the US Dollar between the time you list your item, and the item your item is paid for. Start getting familiar with exchange rates at http://xe.com which offers free realtime exchange rates.

Many US sellers may get their feet wet by offering to ship only to Canada and the UK. That is fairly understandable. Both countries have a history of being America's closest allies. In addition to discussing shipping to these two countries, I will also discuss my experiences shipping to other countries. Understanding the potential risks associated with shipping to certain countries will help you to decide if shipping to a particular country is worth the risk for you.

6 OUR CLOSE NEIGHBOR & ALLY: CANADA

Canada in general, has a very similar culture to the US while the US shares similar roots with the UK. Other than Quebec (which, from my experience, can be a whole different story), both countries are English-speaking.

On its surface, selling to Canada is an excellent idea. In recent years, the Canadian Dollar has strengthened against the US Dollar. The Canadian Dollar is often at par with the US Dollar. From time to time, it may even be worth *more* than the US Dollar. The cost of living in Canada is generally higher than in the US so the average Canadian is used to paying more for items compared to the average American.

Unfortunately, there are a few issues that work against you when you sell to Canada:

- Many American items are also widely available in Canada - no arbitrage opportunities there.

- Many US sellers will ship to Canada. Why not? It's a safe bet and shipping to Canada is quite similar to simply shipping within the US. The "less competition" advantage is diminished when you are selling to the Canadian market.

- Finally, I believe the biggest problem with trying to sell to Canadians is their high import taxes. Canadian buyers seem to be very wary of buying anything across borders for the fear of being hit with a high import tax.

In my nearly two decades of selling on eBay, and in all my many thousands of items shipped all over the world, my shipments to Canada have been a drop in the bucket.

If you want to sell specifically to Canadians, you can consider selling on ebay.ca. I have not experienced any surge or improvement in Canadian sales by listing on http://ebay.ca. The only time that I saw an increase in Canadian buyers was when I was on an extended vacation in Canada and was shipping items from within Canada.

By no means am I saying that you should disregard your potential Canadian market. However, I would not count on Canada as being a big share of your international market.

Possible Issues With A Canadian Order/Buyer

Dealing with an average Canadian buyer should be little different from dealing with an average American one. Just be sure that you are clear in your listing that Canada will impose import taxes on any orders that you are shipping from the US. The price does not include Canadian taxes and they are responsible for paying those taxes to their local authorities.

Shipping to Canada

In general, problems with loss or damage while shipping to Canada is unlikely. You should bear in mind that even though Canada is just across the border, you should not assume that shipping to Canada will take approximately the same time frame as shipping across the US.

On the contrary, it can take as long as 4-6 weeks for a shipment to reach Canada compared to about 1-2 weeks to ship a package across the US. I have no explanation for this distance versus time discrepancy, other than it is my guess that Canadian customs a long time to process shipments.

The longer end of the shipping time frame usually applies to shipments sent to Quebec. From my experience, French-speaking countries/regions seem to take the longest time to deliver shipments. The reason is unknown to me.

7 "It's the Economy, Stupid" -- The UK

Shipping to the UK is the next great international selling leap for many American sellers. I believe that US seller receptiveness to shipping to the UK is similar to their reasons for selling to Canada. Do not get me wrong, selling to the British is a great idea.

In fact, the UK market was a large part of my business when I started selling on eBay in the late 1990s. The British Pound then was extremely strong and good profits were to be made by simply taking advantage of currency differences beneficial to me.

Unfortunately however, the UK economy had already started to slow from 1997-2008. Like the US, the UK has been hit by the 2008 Great Recession. According to Wikipedia, "A report released by the Office for National Statistics on 14 May 2013 revealed that over the six-year period between 2005 and 2011, the UK dropped from 5th place to 12th place in terms of household income on an international scale — the drop was partially attributed to the devaluation of sterling over this time frame." Yes - the decline of the value of the British Pound means that it is now less advantageous to sell in Pound Sterling.

Moreover, since 2008, unemployment in the UK has jumped by over 3%. Additionally, according to ForecastChart.com (http://bit.ly/1obpOsD), the British Pound has lost 9% of its value against the US Dollar in the past decade.

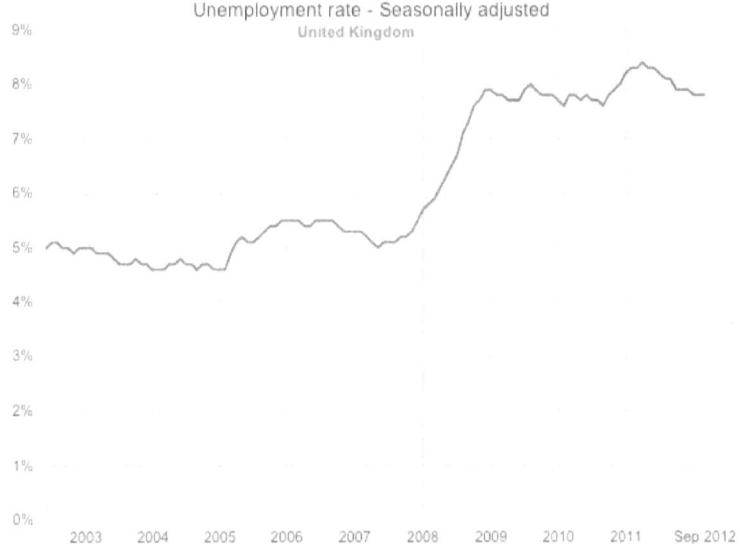

"Unemployment rate in the United Kingdom, seasonally adjusted, September 2002-2012" is copyright (c) 2013 UKecongraphsup and made available under a Attribution-Share Alike 3.0 Unported license.

What that means for you as the US eBay seller is that a shrinking UK economy equals fewer buyers willing to pay more. A lower valued British Pound means you will get less US Dollars after currency conversion. Still, even though it is not as attractive as before, I believe that the British market is still a fairly viable market.

How to Sell to the British Market

If you want to target the British market, you will need to do more than just include offering to ship to the British Isles. eBay makes your listings "invisible" to UK buyers who search in ebay.co.uk. In order for your http://ebay.com listings to show up on http://ebay.co.uk, you will need to check the "eBay UK visibility" box. There is an additional listing fee for this visibility "service". Your listing will then show up in ebay.com.uk searches, with your price automatically showing up to UK buyers in Pound Sterling (£) based on the current exchange rate.

The price in the search will be italicized to indicate that the listing is not originally listed in £. When the UK buyer clicks on your listing, your item price will be shown in the original US Dollar listing, with a smaller price below it showing the approximate price in £ according to the current exchange rate.

If you really want to specifically target the UK market, I recommend that you list your items directly on http://ebay.co.uk. Your listing will then be listed and shown in £. You can also opt to make your listing show up on http://ebay.com for an additional listing fee. If you are listing on eBay UK, I do not think it's necessary to spend the extra listing fee for the listing to show up on ebay.com.

If you want to target the UK buyer, just have your listing show up to UK buyers. I have found that listing on ebay.co.uk increases sales to the UK much more than simply opting for the "UK visibility" option for the extra fee.

Possible Issues With A UK Order/Buyer

Since English is a common language, as long as you describe your item and your listing terms and conditions clearly, you should have no problems with the average UK buyer. Like Canada, the UK charges import taxes so be sure that your buyer is aware that you are in the US, the item ships from the US and they are responsible for any VAT and/or import taxes incurred. This is especially important if you are listing on http://ebay.co.uk. Not all buyers pay attention to the full listing so it is wise to add an additional informational alert in your listing.

Unlike Canada however, you have to be careful with what you sell to the UK (and outside North America in general). Voltages, plugs, cellphone bandwidths and video formats are all different in the UK. For example, the UK (and almost all Commonwealth countries) use 230V versus 120V in North America.

With regards to TV and game consoles, UK uses PAL rather than NTSC like in North America. DVD, Blu-Ray, Xbox 360 and Nintendo DS are all usually regionally coded and may not be playable outside North America because of the regional coding. Make sure that your buyer is aware that yours is a US-item and that they need to make sure the item is capable before buying.

Also bear in mind that UK is 5-8 hours ahead of US time. So if you are on the West Coast for example, noon West Coast time will be around 8pm UK time. Be prepared for questions and Best Offers (if applicable,) to come to you at more unusual hours because of the time difference.

There is an additional risk-factor if you list your item in £ (or any other currency) - currency fluctuations. Again rewards come with risk. You can potentially make more money than expected if the Pound Sterling strengthens against the US

Dollar in the time between your listing and the time your buyers pays for your item. Conversely, if the Pound Sterling weakens in that time-frame, your profit will be reduced as well.

Shipping to the UK

Other than your package possibly being held up by UK customs, shipping to the UK should be relatively hassle-free. Regular first class airmail via USPS is the cheapest international shipping option for packages under 6 lbs.

Unless there is a festive season rush or there is a UK postal strike (strikes do not seem to be uncommon in the UK), your shipment should reach its UK destination in about 2-3 weeks on average. I have not experienced any problems with unusual postal loss rates for shipments to the UK.

8 A ROAD LESS TRAVELED: AUSTRALIA

Many US sellers overlook a big English-speaking market: Australia. I have to admit that in my earlier eBay selling years, in the late 1990s, I overlooked Australia as well because the Australian Dollar was so much weaker than other currencies.

My views on selling to Australia has since changed. In fact, for 3 years, selling new-release DVDs to Australia was the bread and butter of my eBay business. The Australian Dollar at that time was worth more than the US Dollar and the Australians were willing to pay AU$50 (approximately US$55 at currency exchange rates of that period) on average for a new DVD release that cost me about US$15 to purchase at retail.

To be honest, I am not sure why the Australian were willing to pay so much. I can only assume that it cost a lot to buy DVDs in Australia, and many movies that were released on DVD in the US were just released in theatres in Australia, resulting in demand because of the novelty of have the DVD or movie before everyone else.

In the past 10 years, the Australian Dollar has strengthened against the US Dollar by 23%. According to Wikipedia, "In April 2012, the International Monetary Fund predicted that Australia would be the best-performing major advanced economy in the world over the next two years.

Additionally, according to the 2011 Credit Suisse Global Wealth report, Australia has a median wealth of US$222,000

(US$217,559), the highest in the world and nearly four times the amount of each US adult. The proportion of those with wealth above US$100,000 is the highest of any country – eight times the world average. Average wealth was US$397,000, the world's second-highest after Switzerland."

Do not ignore the Australian market! The strong Australian Dollar, its strong economy, higher cost of living, strong buying power, reliable postal service, large English-speaking population and its penchant for American pop culture makes Australia and very viable market.

A Distinct Advantage: Amazon Is Not Yet in Australia

Besides most US sellers overlooking the Australian market, selling to Australia also presents one other distinct advantage - at the time of writing, Amazon.com has not yet cracked into the Australian market.

Sure, they sell Kindles and Kindle books on amazon.com.au but they are not selling physical goods in Australia. At least not yet. Get *your* stuff to Australia before Amazon does!

I recommend listing items directly on http://ebay.com.au for maximum Australian exposure. Your listings will be in AU$. I have found that sales to Australia for listings on ebay.com in US$ with shipping to Australia are marginal at best compared to listings placed on eBay Australia.

Possible Issues With An Australian Order/Buyer

I have never had any problems that were out of the ordinary when dealing with an Australian buyer. Again, be aware that Australian systems are for the most part, based on British systems so any electronic compatibility issues would be similar to those that may arise with a UK buyer.

As long as you are clear, there should not be any problems. From my experience, Australians generally know what they are buying and getting into when they buy from a US seller.

Again, remember that Australia is about 14 hours ahead of the US in time (depending on where you are in the US vs Australia). That means their daytime is our nighttime. Expect questions and Best Offers (if applicable,) to come to you at unusually odd hours. The nice thing about selling on ebay.com.au however, is that you literally sell while you sleep! It is exciting to see a boost in funds in your Paypal account first thing in the morning!

Australia is also in the Southern Hemisphere so that means the seasons compared to American seasons are reversed. Our summertime is their wintertime, our springtime is their fall. As a US-based eBay seller, you could potentially buy seasonal clearance clothing in the US to sell to Australians, where the season is just starting.

I have never tried selling seasonal clothing to Australia because I find selling clothes on eBay in general to be too much of a hassle. It might be something that could work for you though.

Shipping to Australia

Shipping to Australia during non-festive season usually takes 2-3 weeks to arrive. I have found the Australian Post to be very reliable. In fact, I do not recall suffering any shipment losses in all my years of shipping to Australia, which is impressive.

At the time of writing, Australia does not charge import tax for shipments under AU$1000. This is a high threshold so most eBay sellers should not run into any tariff problems with shipments to Australia.

9 AFFLUENT NON ENGLISH-SPEAKING EUROPE

I have to admit that while I have eyed markets in the rest of Europe, I have had trouble cracking into them because of language barriers. I have tried listing items on eBay Germany (http://ebay.de), eBay France (http://ebay.fr), eBay Netherlands (http://ebay.nl), eBay Italy and eBay Ireland.

While eBay Ireland is in English, I have found sales to be poor. I have found that selling on http://ebay.co.uk bring me more Irish customers than selling on http://ebay.ie.

Of all the eBay European markets, I think the best market to focus on outside of ebay UK is eBay Germany. Its large, affluent population with a high cost of living makes the market very attractive. At present, Germany is the world's fourth largest economy and is one of eBay's biggest markets. What has worked best for me has been to simply list items on ebay.com and offer worldwide shipping.

Possible Issues With An European Order/Buyer

Many Europeans, especially those shopping on directly at ebay.com will be able to write or understand at least some English. Other than potential language barriers, the issues you will likely encounter with an European buyer (excluding Italians), will be similar to those you experience with a British buyer.

A special note on Italy: In my nearly two decades of shipping all over the world, the shipping destination that I have experienced the most problems with have been shipments to Italy. Shipping to Italy, for me, has always been very slow and unreliable. A majority of the packages sent to Italy often will get lost/stolen.

I recommend passing on your potential Italian market. I feel that the hassle and risk is too great for a small market. eBay will allow you to pick the countries you will or will not ship to in each auction listing. Just exclude Italy, which will bar anyone registered in Italy from purchasing your item.

If you choose to ship to Italy, consider shipping via Priority Mail or Global Priority Mail which insures your shipment and provides online tracking. Both services are not cheap but may be worth it if you want to sell higher priced items to Italy.

Flat-rate Priority Mail is cheaper but does not allow you to purchase insurance nor does it have international tracking. If you want to insure first class mail or flat-rate Priority Mail packages to Italy, you can also use third-party insurers like U-PIC (http://u-pic.com) or Shipsaver (http://shipsaver.com).

Shipping to Europe

From my experience, shipping during non-festive periods to *most* of Western Europe (including the UK, Germany and Scandinavia) normally takes 2-3 weeks.

Shipping to French-speaking Europe (including France and Belgium) normally takes 4-6 weeks (sometimes more), shipping to Italy (assuming the shipment makes it to its destination,) normally takes 60-90 days, sometimes more.

10 GOING SOUTH: BRAZIL

Brazil has been an unexpected market for me. Before sales started rolling from Brazil, I had never even considered it, or any other country in South America a potential market for me. I simply assumed that the language barrier alone was too much of a problem to even deal with developing economies. Boy, was I wrong. When so many economies around the world crumbled in the Great Recession of 2008, selling to this country helped to shore my sales up: Brazil.

At that time, I did not know what was happening in Brazil but according to Wikipedia, "Brazil's economy is the largest of the Latin American nations and the second largest in the western hemisphere. Brazil is one of the fastest-growing major economies in the world with an average annual GDP growth rate of over 5 percent. In future decades, Brazil is expected to become one of the five largest economies in the world.

According to the World Economic Forum, Brazil was the top country in upward evolution of competitiveness in 2009, gaining eight positions among other countries, overcoming Russia for the first time, and partially closing the competitiveness gap with India and China among the BRIC economies."

As you can see, while American and European markets were in turmoil in 2008-2010, Brazil was booming. That would be a plausible explanation for my new market. Again, I never considered selling to Brazil. However, I did offer worldwide shipping while most US sellers do not. That must have driven

Brazilian buyers to my listings. My big seller to Brazil was video games, because that was my niche at that time. However to me, they were also obviously buying other items because they would also buy kitchen appliances when I listed those. Profits on my sales were not as great as when I was selling DVDs to Australia in a good economy but it was a profit with a consistent market so I decided to take the risk and roll with it.

Possible Issues With A Brazilian Order/Buyer

I have noticed that the Brazilians that I have dealt with could in general, communicate in understandable English. The issues you will encounter will likely be similar to those you would encounter a non-English speaking European buyer.

Shipping to Brazil

Shipping to Brazil is a little scary. Third-party insurers like U-PIC and Shipsaver will *not* insure shipments to Brazil. As far as I know, the only way that you can get your package to Brazil insured is if you ship using USPS global priority or express mail - both of which are very expensive shipping options. By all means, offer it as an option to your buyers.

I took the risk - I have shipped most packages to Brazil uninsured via USPS first class airmail. Shipping times to Brazil is slow - an average of 60 days if not more. My experience with shipping to Brazil is that their mail is semi-reliable. I have had a very small minority of the packages getting lost. I get more shipping losses to Brazil compared to most of Europe, Asia or Australia but losses are far less than shipping to Italy.

11 SELLING ELSEWHERE

I will lump shipping to the rest of the world together. Outside of North America, Australia and Europe, I have shipped to many countries including Russia; Peru, Argentina, Ecuador, Mexico, Chile in Central and South America; Egypt, Saudi Arabia, the United Arab Emirates, Israel, South Africa, Turkey and even Madagascar in Africa and the Middle East; China, India, Taiwan, Hong Kong, Japan, Malaysia, Indonesia, Singapore and Brunei in Asia.

My experiences shipping to these countries are more anecdotal rather than based on any real pattern. In general, shipping to Russia and South America takes about a month, shipping to the Middle East (except Israel) and Madagascar takes about 60-90 days, shipping to Asia and Israel can take anywhere from 2-4 weeks on average. Shipments to Russia are uninsurable through third-party insurers but my experience with the Russian mail so far has been OK.

12 A Japanese Middleman

If you end up selling items that are attractive to the Japanese market, you may inevitably come across a suspicious looking buyer with a "flight2" prefix. According to the company's own account, they purchase on behalf of Japanese buyers under the following IDs:

flight2nrt, flight2sfo, flight2lax, flight2nyc, flight2ord, flight2hnd, flight2cts, flight2fuk, flight2kix, flight2bos

They basically serve as a middleman for Japanese buyers who want to buy items from the US but are unable or unwilling to do so. Instead, they use SAA who has a US receiving address.

Using SAA, these buyers can then order items from sellers that may only ship within the US. The US seller ships to SAA's California address and SAA in turn forwards the package to the buyer in Japan.

SAA got my fraud senses up when they first bought one of my items. They have an unusual buying activity and no selling activity. Their paypal shipping address is to a company called "SHOP AIRLINES AMERICA" (SAA) in California.

I read quite a few complaints online of fraud by company but I have dealt with them a few times without any problems. To prevent any problems, do as they instruct: write the item# of their order clearly in bold marker on a few sides of the package so that they know what the item is.

13 THE LANGUAGE BARRIER

I suggest that you do not list in another language unless you are capable of doing so. Just leave a translator to do the work for you. You can add a translator app to your listings at http://ebay.to/1rOQ8Ds. The app costs $0.99/month to subscribe to but can come in handy with your non-English speaking potential customers come a knocking. If they ask questions in another language, drop the question into your translator and answer back in English.

Chances are that your buyer will then drop your answer into a translator to figure things out. If the translation ends up garbled, apologize to your buyer (in English) and explain that the translation doesn't make sense, would it be possible for him/her to ask the question in English? Often, the buyer can write a little English.

14 CURRENCY RISK

Sell on a foreign eBay site will generally mean that you will be selling your item in another currency. Currency fluctuations will add an additional element of risk to your listings so make sure you have healthy profit margins to help you ride out any potential currency devaluations against the US$. I cannot predict how currencies are going to behave. If I could, I would be uber rich now!

There is a way, however, that you can insulate yourself slightly against minute to minute fluctuations. When you sell something in another currency, the buyer will send the paypal payment in that currency. When that happens, paypal will ask you if you want the funds converted to US$, or if you want to open a currency account in that currency. I recommend opening a currency account, which will keep that payment in the currency it was paid in.

You can also open a new currency account in your paypal account without needing to first receive a foreign currency payment. On the right of your paypal balance, there is a button that says "Currency converter".

How to Make Money on eBay - International Sales

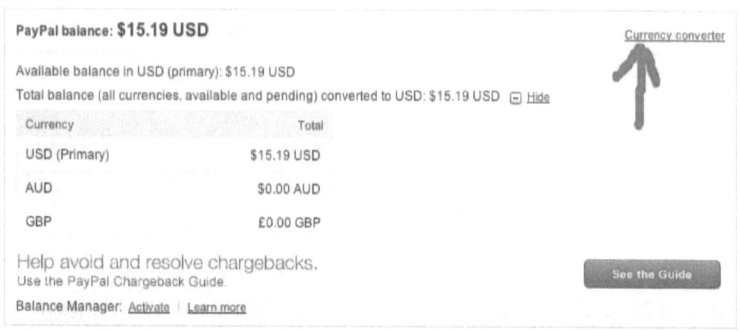

The button will lead you to a new page asking you what currency you want to add to your account. Choose the currency you want (this would normally be AU$, GBP, C$ but it can be any of the currencies you want from that list).

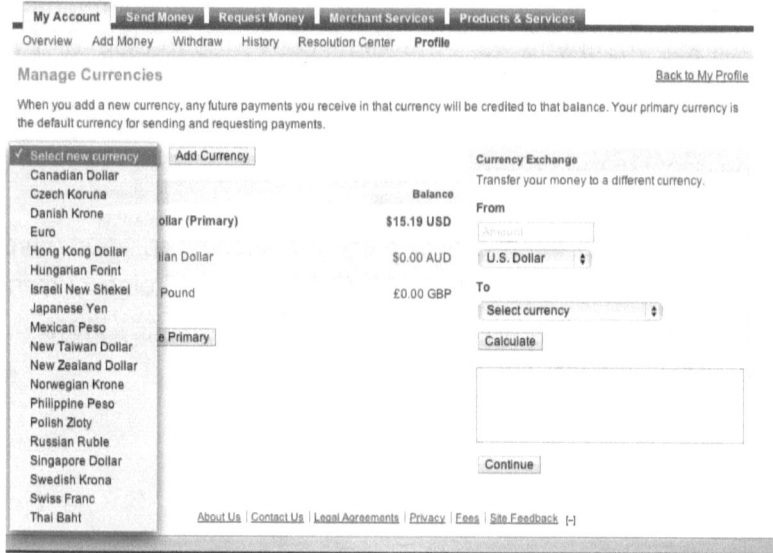

On the right side, you can see how much that currency converted to in US$ based on the current rates. Bear in mind that paypal will charge you a currency conversion fee, which is normally about $0.05 per dollar *less* than actual rates listed at http://xe.com. **Keep this 5% paypal cost in mind when you are figuring out your profit margins based on rates listed on xe.com.**

By keeping your payment in the currency it was paid in, you can insulate yourself from the minute to minute currency fluctuations. That means that you do not need to accept the exchange rate at the exact time that the buyer sent payment. If the rates are not favorable at that time, you can choose to not exchange it until you get a better rate. If they are good, you should convert the funds immediately.

I have had held funds for a long as over a year, waiting for more favorable rates. The wait can mean a difference of and additional 20-30% in profits. Of course, a currency can drop against the US$ for an extended period of time for any number of reasons. How long you want to hold the funds in another currency will depend on how liquid you want to be, and on your risk appetite.

15 Fraud Risk

There is always the risk of fraud, whether you are selling domestically or internationally. However, I think the main high-fraud areas include parts of Africa and Indonesia. While I have shipped a few items to Indonesia without a hitch, ship with caution.

Based on my experience, I believe there is a higher fraud rate when dealing with Indonesian buyers. This is especially the case if you are dealing with higher-priced electronics and cameras (anything about US$50). I do not recommend offering to ship high-fraud items to countries other than the "safer" developed-country destinations.

You can lower your risks by nipping it in the bud. A big fraud signal to me, especially when it is from a buyer in a questionable country, is when a buyer needs the order urgently and asks you to ship immediately.

If you do decide to ship to Indonesia or parts of Africa, hold on to the shipment for a few days so see if Paypal catches any fraud activity. Sometimes Paypal will hold a payment from a questionable transaction. If this happens, just tell Paypal to cancel the transaction and call it your lucky day.

The urgent request "fraud alert" may not apply if it is a customer in a developed country and it is between October and mid December - during the Christmas rush. In these cases, use your discretion in accepting the order and request.

16 Shipping Logistics & Risk

Packages that enter a foreign will have to pass through customs. If you're labelling your shipments by hand, packages will have to be accompanied by the international customs form which you stick onto your package. At the time of writing, the USPS has a three-piece form, with a self-adhesive green label that you affix on the package. Your local post office can give you the correct form that you need.

You will need to add both yours and your addressee's addresses on the form. You will also need to declare the contents of the package, as well as its value. Your package will probably get returned by the destination country's customs if you do not have this form affixed to the package.

If you are printing shipping labels via eBay, you will not need to fill the green USPS customs label. The customs form will generate together with your shipping label and postage in one handy shipping label.

To reduce their tax liability, some buyers in these countries may ask you to mark their package as "GIFT" rather than "MERCHANDISE". I do not suggest lying. Just mark it "MERCHANDISE" just to be safe. I do however, put the price of what *I* paid for the item in the package "VALUE" section of the customs form.

Sorry, but I am not going to mark an unused Myanmarese airline barf bag as being worth $50 because one lone buyer was willing to pay that insane amount for it. Many items I sell are free items so the value I put down is $0.

You can help to lower your shipment theft risk by describing your package contents in a less attractive manner. For example, if you titled your eBay listing as "Vintage Dragonball Toy - Rare and Hard to Find", that auction title will appear as so in the customs label. That description may make the package more susceptible to theft enroute. Instead, change the customs form declaration to state "Old Toy".

Similarly, instead of stating on the customs form that the item is a "Brand new GUCCI Bag", just state, "Bag" on your form - this makes it a lot less attractive sounding. Mark the value as low as possible without outright lying. The higher the value stated on your customs form, the higher your risk of the item getting stolen.

Stating a lowered value will not affect your insured value. The insurance value is what you state when you purchase insurance. If your insurer account is connected to your eBay listing, the insured amount is sometimes automatically calculated when you purchase it. The customs valuation is a separate amount that you list in your customs declaration. At the time of writing, the two are independent.

Postal Loss and Insurance

In you ship across the world, there will be an increased risk of package loss or damage - the odds are not in your favor. The greater the distance your package has to ship, the more hands your package has to pass through, the higher your risk of the package getting lost or damaged.

Thankfully, in all my years of selling, the international postal system has proven itself to be fairly safe. Almost all packages do end up safely with the buyer. Shipments to Canada, Western Europe (except Italy), the UK, most of Asia (Japan, Thailand, Singapore), Australia and New Zealand all have pretty reliable postal systems. I have not experienced any real problems shipping to these countries.

The USPS only offers insurance options on items shipped via non-flat rate Priority Mail or Express Mail. However, you can also purchase insurance on most USPS international first class package shipments through third party providers like U-PIC (http://u-pic.com) or Shipsaver (http://shipsaver.com).

I have used both and the process for purchasing and making claims is easier than USPS's insurance which is a pain to file claims through. Both companies' rates are also lower than the USPS's insurance rates. The downside is that they will not insure shipments to every country. Destination countries they will not insure include Brazil and Russia.

These are the main issues I have encountered with international shipping. It is up to you to decide if your profit is worth the risk.

eBay Global Shipping Program

If you are still leary of shipping internationally, eBay now has a service called the Global Shipping Program. I have never used this service because I would then lose out on the opportunity to pad my profits a little through shipping charges.

To qualify, you have to be a US seller with standard or better rating. You simply charge the buyer the cost of shipping your package to eBay's US shipping facility which will then re-ship your package to the international location for you (they will take care of the customs forms etc).

The buyer is charged the appropriate additional fees in their final price. They will also be informed of the amount charged by you and the amount charged by the facility to have the item shipped to them. eBay will only charge you their commission on the domestic shipping charges you specified. Joining the program is free and you will not have to bear the risk of loss or damage after the package arrives at the facility. You can refer to http://ebay.to/1okMFSv for more information.

17 Describing Your Item for an International Sale

There are a few things you need to add in your auction listing that will help to prevent problems arising from miscommunication. If you are selling on a non-English market especially and you are not fluent in that language, list your item in English and include the translator.

Also state clearly that you do not understand German or French or Portuguese etc. Ask the buyer to please use English if possible, or if not possible, to please use the translator and you will do the same in your communication.

If you are listing in an English-speaking foreign eBay site like eBay UK or eBay Australia, be clear that the item is in the US and ships from the US. I also recommend including in all relevant listings that your item is a US item. The buyer is responsible for making sure that they can run or play the item in their country. I do not issue refunds of incompatibility problems.

If your listing is on ebay.com and you are offering to ship internationally, you can state something like this: "While I will ship this item internationally, please be aware that this is a US item. I do not know if this item will work in your country. Buyer is responsible to ensuring that the item will work in their country before buying as no refunds will be issued for problems arising from incompatibility."

Customs

At the time of writing, most Asian countries and Australia do not change import taxes on items below a certain value. However, many countries including Canada, the UK, most of Scandinavia and Brazil charge their residents import taxes.

I do not know what the value thresholds are before each country levies their tax. That means that your buyer may have additional fees levied on their order. I suggest adding an advisory in your auction listings. Most buyers in these countries are aware of their country's import taxes but I like to err on the side of caution.

In all of my auctions, I state something like this: **"I will ship internationally, however, the buyer is responsible for all customs/import taxes which their country may impose. The price of shipping this item does not include any of these taxes. I do not know if or what those taxes are. Please consult your local authorities for more information before purchasing."**

If you like, you can include this free trial Duty Calculator service in your listings (http://bit.ly/1vzuitq) so that your buyers can check the estimated duties for themselves. I have never used this service and cannot attest to the accuracy of their calculations.

Specifying Shipping Time Estimates

Shipping times - as long as you advise your customers of shipping time frames, I've found that international customers are pretty understanding of the time lags. I believe a bulk of shipping times are because something got stuck in customs.

You should place your notice right in your auction description. Make sure that your customer understands that international delivery times can vary greatly depending on country, region and time of year. Packages can be held up significantly going through customs.

Here is an example of what you can include in your description:

"Please note that item ships from USA. On average, shipping to France/Belgium takes 4-6 weeks, shipping to Italy takes 90+ days, shipping to most of Asia, Australia, UK and most of other parts of Western Europe takes 2-3 weeks.

Shipping to Canada usually takes about a month and shipping to Brazil normally takes 60+ days. These are just guidelines. unfortunately, I am not able to predict how long a package will take to reach you."

Of course, there are other variables which include where you are shipping from, where you are shipping to, and the time of year you're shipping. For example, if you're shipping from Los Angeles, CA, your packages will leave the country faster as compared to my packages which are sent from my Colorado mountain town to Denver (takes at least 1 day) before it makes its ground trek to LA or some other port city (which can take 3-5 days,) before leaving the country. Similarly, a package sent to a major hub like London will reach its addressee much faster than if it has to make its way slowly from London to a small town in rural England.

Finally, the time of year you ship can make a big difference in both domestic and international delivery times. Expect shipping times to increase especially before a big festive season like Christmas. Christmas is also when packages have an arrival date line and when customers get impatient. I suggest advising international customers that Christmas presents that do not ship at least a month (6 weeks if you want to be extra safe,) before Christmas may not arrive in time.

18 Conclusion

I hope I have covered all the potential benefits and pitfalls of selling internationally. I have shipped the most mundane and the oddest items all over the world. Not only have I increased my profit margins by doing so, it is a blast to see some of my silliest items being sent to some of the most exotic locations.

If you are still afraid, start with a few smaller, cheaper items. Or get your feet wet selling chocolate chips! Go on and take the plunge. I will be here cheering you on.

Sign up for my newsletter and get THREE books for free:

HOW TO KEEP BACKYARD CHICKENS
CAN DOS & DON'TS
THE MODERN AMERICAN FRUGAL HOUSEWIFE BOOK

Click here to get started: http://byjillb.com

Books By Jill b.

Please check out my other books at http://byjillb.com:

The Modern Frugal American Housewife Book #1
Home Economics

The Modern Frugal American Housewife Book #2
Organic Gardening

The Modern Frugal American Housewife Book #3
Moms Edition

The Modern Frugal American Housewife Book #4
Emergency Prepping

How to Keep Backyard Chickens
A Straightforward Beginner's Guide

The Best Backyard Chicken Breeds
A List of Top Birds for Pets, Eggs and Meat

Foraging
A Beginner's Guide to Wild Edible and Medicinal Plants

Medicinal Herb Garden
10 Plants for the Self-Reliant Homestead Prepper

Hidden
Prepper's Secret Edible Garden

CAN Dos and Don'ts
Water Bath and Pressure Canning

How to Make Money on eBay: Beginner's Guide
From Setting Up Accounts to Selling Like a Pro

How to Make Money on eBay: Maximize Profits
Secrets, Stories, Tips and Hacks - Confessions of a 16-Year eBay Veteran

How to Make Money on eBay: International Sales
Taking the Fear and Guesswork Out of Doing Business Internationally on eBay

Self-Publish on a Budget with Amazon
A Guide for the Author Publishing eBooks on Kindle

About the Author

~ Self-Reliance: One Step at a Time ~
http://byjillb.com

With a no-nonsense style, Jill Bong draws from her own homesteading experiences and mistakes, and writes books focusing on maximizing output with minimal input to save you time and money.

Jill writes under the pen name Jill b. She is an author, entrepreneur, homesteader and is the co-inventor and co-founder of Chicken Armor (http://chickenarmor.com), an affordable, low maintenance chicken saddle. She has also written over a dozen books on homesteading and self-reliance.

Jill has been mentioned/quoted in various publications including The Associated Press, The New York Times, The Denver Post and ABC News. She has written for various magazines including Countryside and Small Stock Journal, Molly Green, Farm Show Magazine and Backyard Poultry Magazine. She holds an Engineering degree from an Ivy League from a previous life.

At its height, her previous homestead included over 100 chickens, geese and ducks, as well as cats, a dog, bees and a donkey named Elvis. She currently learning permaculture techniques to apply to her homestead in rural Oregon. Learn more by visiting her site http://byjillb.com.

Disclaimer & Disclosure: This guide is for entertainment and informational purposes only. The author and anyone associated with this book shall not be held liable for damages incurred through the use of information provided herein. Content included on this book is not intended to be, nor does it constitute, the giving of health, financial, legal or professional advice.

The author and others associated with this book make no representation as to the accuracy, completeness or validity of any information in this book. While every caution has been taken to provide the most accurate information, please use your own discretion before making any decisions based solely on the content herein. The author and others associated with this book are not liable for any errors or omissions nor will provide any form of compensation if you suffer an inconvenience, loss or damages of any kind because of, or by making use of, the information contained herein. If in doubt, always seek the advice of a professional who can advise you appropriately before acting on any part of this book.

This book contains references and links to other Third Party products and services. Some of these references have been included for the convenience of the readers and to make the book more complete. They should not be construed as endorsements from, or of any of these Third Parties or their products or services. These links and references may contain products and opinions expressed by their respective owners. The author does not assume liability or responsibility for any Third Party material or opinions.

www.ingramcontent.com/pod-product-compliance
Lightning Source LLC
Chambersburg PA
CBHW030704190526
45164CB00004B/381